The Dragonfly Door

Written by John Adams
Illustrated by Barbara L. Gibson

FEATHER ROCK BOOKS, INC.
MAPLE PLAIN, MINNESOTA

A Note from the Author and Publisher

THIS STORY about two insect friends, Lea and Nym, was written to help parents express their views about life and death.

Because young minds are impressionable, we recommend that a parent or other responsible adult read this book first to determine its suitability for individual children.

A child who has experienced a loss similar to Nym's needs both time to heal and positive support from family and friends. In some instances, counseling may be needed.

For readers who want to know more about nymphs and dragonflies, some general facts are included at the end of the book.

For additional resources or to comment on this book, please visit our Web site at *www.featherrockbooks.com.*

Published by Feather Rock Books, Inc. – Maple Plain, Minnesota
Text copyright © 2007 by Feather Rock Books, Inc.
Illustrations copyright © 2007 by Feather Rock Books, Inc.

For further information write to:
Feather Rock Books, Inc.
P.O. Box 99
Maple Plain, MN 55359

1-952-473-9091

For additional copies of this book, please visit your local bookstore
or our Web site at *www.featherrockbooks.com.*

First U.S. Paperback Edition
16 15 14 13 12   1 2 3 4 5

Manufactured in the United States of America
by Worzalla in Stevens Point, Wisconsin
December 2012, Job number 324759
ISBN: 978-1-934066-16-4 (paperback)

Publisher's hardcover edition cataloged as follows:
(Provided by Quality Books, Inc.)

    Adams, John, 1960-
        The dragonfly door / written by John Adams ; illustrated by Barbara L. Gibson. — Rev. 1st ed.
        p. cm.
        SUMMARY: Two insect friends, water nymphs Lea and Nym, play together in the marsh.
    While sleeping, Nym discovers that her friend Lea has died and gone to a new world as a dragonfly.
        Audience: Ages 5-9.
        LCCN 2006911214
        ISBN-13: 978-1-934066-12-6
        ISBN-10: 1-934066-12-5

        1. Death—Juvenile fiction. 2. Future life—Juvenile fiction. 3. Friendship—Juvenile fiction.
    4. Dragonflies—Juvenile fiction. [1. Death—Fiction. 2. Future life—Fiction. 3. Friendship—Fiction.
    4. Dragonflies—Fiction. 5. Insects—Fiction.] I. Gibson, Barbara, ill. II. Title.

    PZ7.A2139Dra 2007   [E]
            QBI06-700304

In memory of Hans

For Anne, who offers hope to grieving families
For Mom and Dad, who live in my heart
Also for Chris, Andrew, Jeff, Abby and Clea,
whom I love dearly
– JA

For my family, who have always sought
and found answers in nature
– BLG

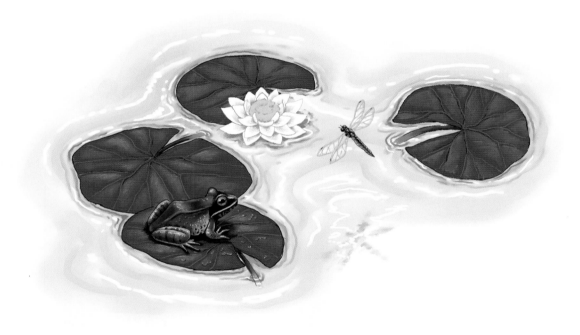

It was a warm spring day in the marsh. Beetles and minnows darted through the reeds.

Two small nymphs, Lea and Nym, zigzagged between the rocks underwater.

"I'm going to catch you!" Nym shouted.

"Oh, no, you're not!" Lea laughed.

But Lea, being a year older, slowed down just enough for Nym to catch up.

"Tag, you're it!" Nym squealed as she poked Lea with one of her legs.

The two friends stopped to rest on a smooth black rock.
"I love to play tag, especially with you," Nym said.
"Me, too," Lea replied. "But I'm getting tired. Let's go home."
Nym was almost two years old. Lea was three. Both had hatched from tiny eggs. Like all water nymphs, though, they never knew their parents. Their moms and dads had moved on after hiding the eggs in some reeds.

Nym and Lea had met in the water meadow. They soon became friends and decided to move in together. Their home was a small nest of leaves and twigs beneath the ledge of a rock.

They played together every day. Afterward, Lea, being the oldest, always reminded Nym to scrub the mud from her legs.

"Remember, we don't want mud in the nest," she would say. "And before you go outside again, would you straighten the leaves and twigs on your side of the bed?"

Sometimes Nym thought Lea treated her like a baby. In fact, the morning after their game of tag, Nym screamed so loud her voice cracked. "Lea, quit telling me what to do! I know I'm supposed to keep mud out of the nest. I wish you would just leave me alone!"

"Nym, please," Lea said in a soft voice. "I just want you to help keep the nest clean."

But Nym left in a huff and swam to the smooth black rock to play tag with the newborn tadpoles.

"You won't believe how bossy Lea can be," she told them.

Nym spent hours chasing the tadpoles from one side of the rock to the other.

"I love this game!" she squealed. She didn't feel angry at Lea anymore.

Meanwhile, Lea decided to swim to the edge of the marsh to look for Nym's favorite water flowers that grow in the tall reeds.

"I feel bad that Nym was so angry with me," Lea said to herself. "The flowers will show her how much I love her."

But as she swam to the reeds, Lea had trouble breathing. She moved very slowly as she made her way to the edge of the marsh.

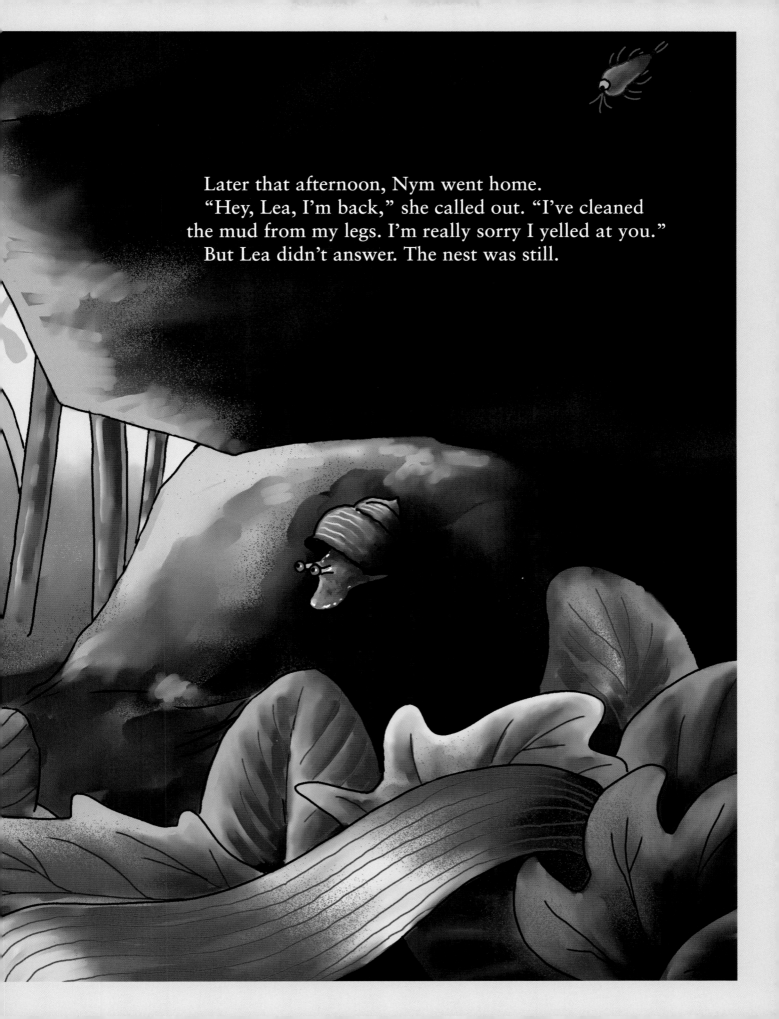

Later that afternoon, Nym went home.
"Hey, Lea, I'm back," she called out. "I've cleaned
the mud from my legs. I'm really sorry I yelled at you."
But Lea didn't answer. The nest was still.

Nym crawled through the nest, looking under the leaves for her friend.

"Lea?" she called again. "Lea, are you here?"

There was still no answer.

Nym's mouth quivered. She went out to search for Lea.

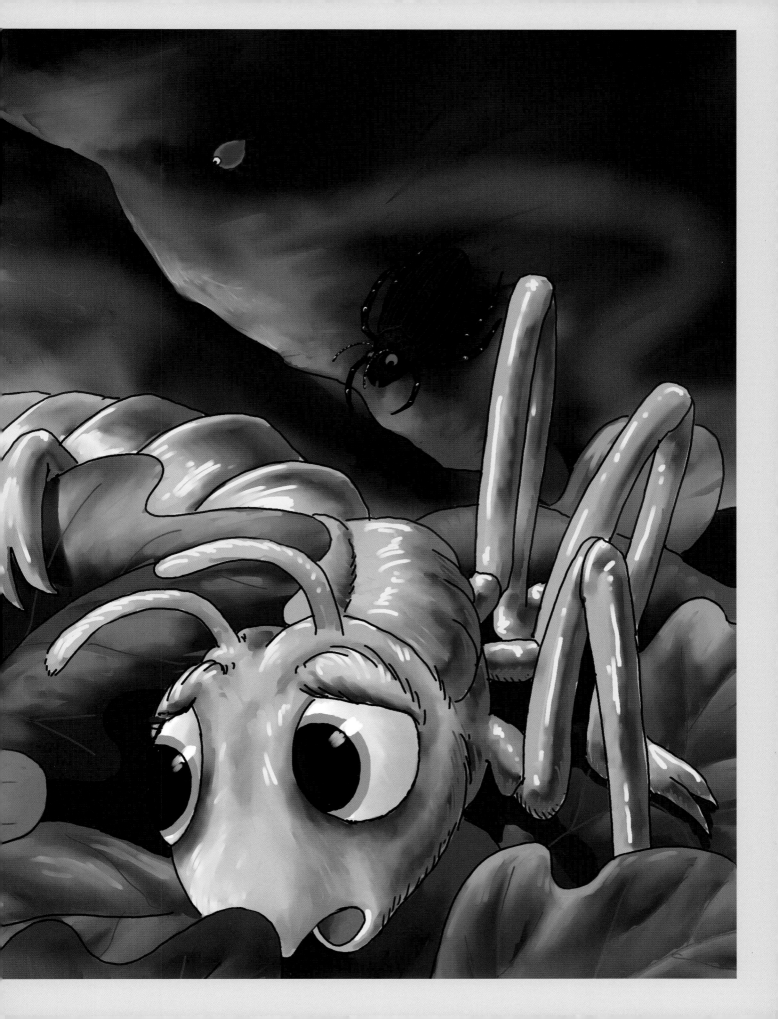

When she saw the Beetle family foraging for food in the grassy weeds, she asked, "Have you seen Lea?"

"Nope, not today," one of the beetles replied.

"I can't find her," Nym said. "If you see her, please tell her I'm looking for her."

The Beetle family nodded their heads and marched off into the weeds.

Nym continued her search, this time in the moss.

She saw the Minnow family playing with empty tadpole eggs. "Have you seen Lea?" she asked.

"Yes, I saw her," the largest minnow called out. "She was on her way to the tall reeds, but swimming very slowly."

"Thanks!" said Nym. "If you see her again, please tell her I'm looking for her."

"Will do," the friendly minnows shouted as they flicked a tadpole egg with their tails.

It was too late in the day for Nym to swim to the edge of the marsh where the tall reeds grow. It would be dark before she got there. "Lea is probably on her way home," she thought. "I'll hurry back to the nest."

But that night, Lea did not
return home and Nym went to
bed in an empty nest for the
first time. She curled up in a
soft leaf that Lea had given her.
   "I'm sorry I yelled at you,"
Nym whispered as she clutched
the leaf. "I miss you."
   Rocking back and forth,
Nym cried herself to sleep.

Early the next morning, a rustling sound startled Nym awake. She quickly rolled back the leaf. "Lea, is that you?"

But it was a family of saucer bugs searching for food.

Nym left the nest in the early daylight and raced to the far edge of the marsh. She searched through the reeds and water flowers all day, but there was no sign of Lea.

Exhausted, Nym clutched one of the reeds and cried.

"Lea, where are you?" she called out as her eyes darted back and forth, scanning the water one more time for her friend. "Please answer, I miss you."

Night fell over the marsh. Cold and alone, Nym fell asleep clinging to the reed.

While Nym slept, she heard Lea's voice saying, "Follow me, Nym. I'm going to show you where I am."

They began to climb, up the reed into the warm light near the water's surface. As they continued to climb, the water mysteriously disappeared, revealing a beautiful new world.

"I died and went to this special place," Lea said, her voice full of love.

"But I didn't want you to leave," Nym pleaded. "I'm sorry I yelled."

"I know you're sorry," Lea assured her. "I left because my water nymph body died while I was picking flowers in the reeds, not because you yelled."

"Will I see you again?" Nym asked.

"Only when it's time for you to die too," Lea replied. "You won't see me in the marsh ever again."

"But how will I find you?" Nym asked.

"I'll find you," Lea said. "But let me show you what I will look like the next time you see me. Here, close your eyes."

Nym closed her eyes.

"Now look at me," Lea said.

Nym opened her eyes and saw a dragonfly whose glass-like wings shimmered in the sun.

"Is that really you?" Nym exclaimed. "You are so beautiful!"

Lea gave her friend a tight hug. "I love you so much," she whispered. "Go back to sleep now, I'll be waiting for you."

Nym woke the next morning with tears in her eyes. She felt the love from her friend's hug deep inside.

She called out, "Lea, was that really you?"

There was no answer.

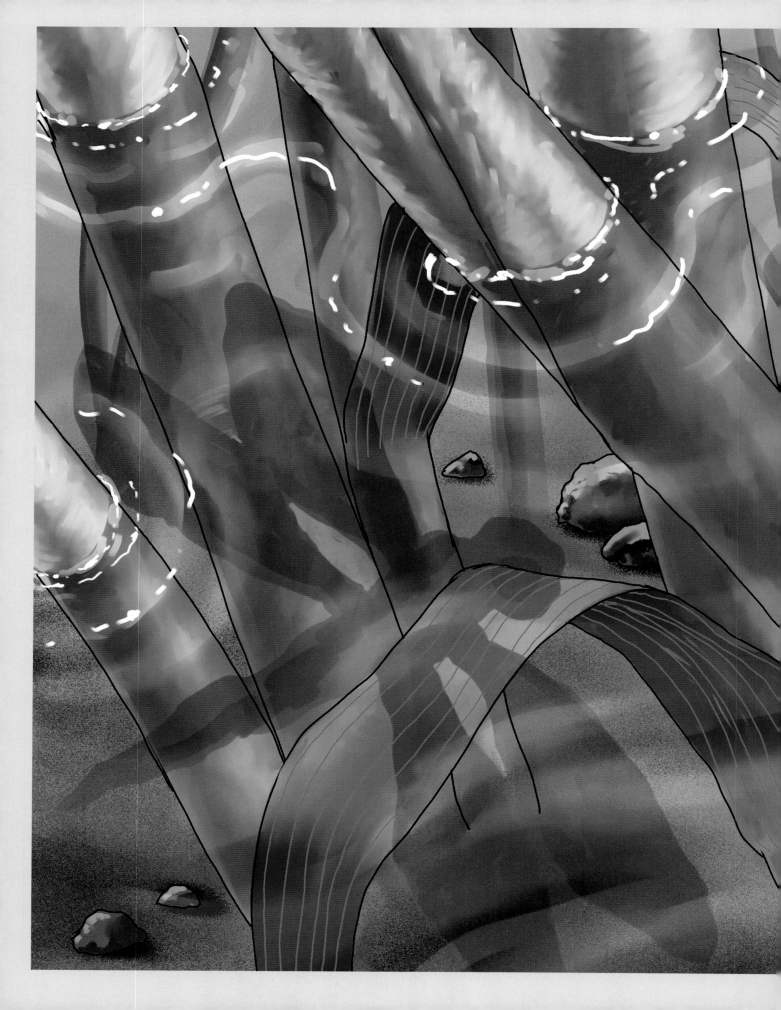

But Nym looked up to where daylight painted the water's surface orange and blue.

She saw a shadow that looked like the shape of a dragonfly. It hovered above her, just beyond the water.

She remembered Lea's voice saying, "I'll be waiting for you."

She looked up again and the shadow disappeared.

Nym was sad for many days. She began to feel better, though, after the Beetle family invited her to live with them. At night, Nym still sleeps with the soft leaf that Lea gave her. Sometimes, before she goes to sleep, she remembers the beautiful dragonfly named Lea. When she thinks about her friend in a special place beyond the marsh, she smiles.

The End

About Nymphs and Dragonflies

THE WATER NYMPHS in this story were young dragonflies.
In real life, a dragonfly usually begins its life in a pond, marsh or stream.

1. DURING THE SUMMER, the mother dragonfly lays her eggs in mud or attaches them to underwater plants. Sometimes she uses her tail to cut into a water plant so she can place her eggs inside. The eggs look like rice-shaped grains of sand.

2. WHEN AN EGG HATCHES, the nymph stays in the water for one to six years. It eats other water creatures and breathes by pumping water through gills in its tail. This pumping also helps it swim fast.

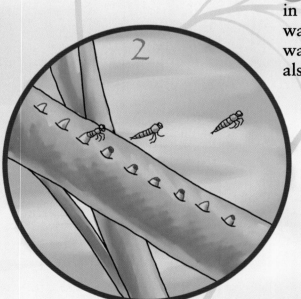

3. AS IT GROWS, the nymph's skin becomes tight and splits open. Each time, though, the nymph crawls out wearing a new larger skin.

7 AN HOUR LATER, it is time to fly and find shelter in tall weeds or trees. Later the dragonfly looks for small insects like mosquitoes to eat. It eventually looks for a partner to help lay eggs.

6 THE MORNING SUN warms the dragonfly. It breathes air and pumps blood through its body to straighten its wrinkled wings.

5 THE NYMPH CLUTCHES the stem and rests above the water. Its skin splits open. But this time, the nymph crawls out as a dragonfly with wings.

4 WHEN READY TO LEAVE the water in the spring and summer, the nymph climbs a stem and emerges into the air. This often happens at night when hungry birds are asleep.